At the Stroke of Midnight
— and —
I'm Still Here
Bamma Ramma Slamma Jamma

MARK IVANCIC

At the Stroke of Midnight And I'm Still Here Bamma
Ramma Slamma Jamma
Copyright © 2019 by Mark Ivancic

Tellwell Talent
www.tellwell.ca

ISBN
978-0-2288-1010-0 (Paperback)

Introduction

An impossibility became a reality on April 25th of this year. I worked out on a daily basis and I was in possibly the best shape in my life I enjoyed life and just loved to play but just like that my world was turned upside down. I had a clot in my neck which moved to my brain.

I used to teach a class called Life Skills, trying to prepare young people for the hardships life may bring them someday. Not realizing I would have to match the talk in the most daunting challenge I have ever had to face.

Tens of thousands of people suffer a stroke in Canada each year impacting hundreds of thousands of Canadians when you include families and friends. Join me as I take you on my personal journey on how a trauma such as this affects someone not just physically but emotionally as well all the way to the top of a mountain ridge in the Canadian Rockies.

I have tried to be honest, hopefully inspirational and at times humorous even though this is no laughing matter. And most importantly of all, I would like this to be a message of hope. And to illustrate the impact in the power of support by loved ones which I was so blessed to experience. I have tried to be all inclusive in thanking all the people who made this trudge (for those who have ever scrambled up a mountain, you can liken this experience to scrambling up loose scree for hundreds and hundreds of metres with no end in sight) doable and if your name didn't make it to print, don't think it means your gesture was any less appreciated or valued.

This ride has been the most arduous battle I have ever faced but, I have tried to put it into words to help those who face the same uphill journey and to give hope to all whose lives are impacted by this experience or any other similar situation. I put the story to rhyme so it could be easy to read and hopefully pleasurable at the same time. I have included some inspirational quotes which I hope inspires the reader regardless of the struggle they are facing.

The main reason for the book was I needed a project to help myself heal and if it helps others, then Bamma Ramma slamma jamma!

At The Stroke of Midnight And I'm Still Here Bam a Ramma Slam a Jamma

It all started on April 25th, 2018,
An event that was totally unforseen,
I played hockey and on my skates I felt so light,
I went for a beer with some buds,
To soak up some suds,
So it was around the stroke of midnight,
When things just didn't feel right,
My head felt like it was going to explode,
So I knew it was time for me to hit the road,
I crept downstairs to the man cave,
Thinking this is how a real man should behave,
 I thought if I closed my eyes and got some sleep that it would
ease the pain,
Not realizing there was something seriously wrong going on
inside my brain,
Looking back not going to the hospital was insane,
And I only have myself to blame,
Because the damage may have been somewhat contained.

Because here is the riddle,
I was kind of young and fit as a fiddle,
Sure I had some belly fat in the middle,
Not a whole lot but there definitely was a little,
I had retired the previous June,
So stress was not a factor,
I was embarking on a new career,
Which had me excited and in good cheer.
I did not smoke so the whole concept of me having a stroke,
Just seemed like some kind of bad joke.

In the morning when my wife saw me,
she knew something was definitely wrong,
My words were slurred, my vision was blurred,
She called for help and the time for the Parkland EMTs to
arrive was not long,
They knew the signs well, and quickly they could tell,
That I had all the symptoms of a stroke,
And all I could think of was this was all some kind of
cosmic joke.
I am 57 and I go to the gym everyday,
Could this actually be happening to me? NO way!
So they hurried me off to the hospital at the U of A.

Sure enough in my head there was a clot,
But the capable staff found it and it was caught,
This can't be happening was my recurring thought.
I spent the next several days in ICU,
Not totally understanding the trauma I was going through,
In the original analysis,
It was determined I suffered left side paralysis,
Trust me that is a scary diagnosis,
And it is as bad as it sounds because my body felt like
a total mess.

In my life skills class, l would give students motivational quotes
such as: "What doesn't kill you only makes you more strong."
But in this case l couldn't be more wrong,
I continually wonder and ask why,
Because no clear explanation can anyone supply,
But I have hopes I found the suspect,
Feeling so good on the night I even did backcheck,
I desperately want someone from the medical profession to tell
me that was my mistake,
And this foolish endeavour I must forsake.

I was in the U of A hospital for two weeks,
Because I was so exceptionally weak,
The nurses were so kind and sweet,
And one in particular was Deb,
Who ensnared me in her kindness web,
She always made me feel like I was a celeb.

'No act of kindness, no matter how small is ever wasted.'
-Aesop

They keep waking me up every couple of hours to test
my cognition,
Asking me the same questions even in the middle of the night,
But I think they keep messing up my information and maybe my
answers they should write,
So in an attempt to keep things light...
"What is your name?" "Clark Kent."
"Where are you?" "In a room filled with kryptonite!"
I can see them questioning that maybe my head is not quite right.
In my life skills class, l would give students motivational quotes
such as: "What doesn't kill you only makes you more strong."
But in this case l couldn't be more wrong,

I have to get a needle and I am asked if I would prefer the left or right side,
Of course I say the left figuring it was fried,
I jump up and wince when it is applied,
My daughter laughs because I was acting wise, but I take it in stride,
Because it means I can still feel on the left side,
And it means there is reason for hope that is justified.

So what's with the "Bamma Ramma Slamma Jamma"?
I would say that in front of students when I was excited,
And when I did, they would be delighted,
So that's all it took to get it ignited.

In a previous life I used to teach,
The children's hearts I tried to reach,
Positivity, kindness and hard work I would preach,
I enjoyed every student... all of you each,
So many warm memories like a sunny day on a beach.

I go to my first physiotherapy session with Jo and Ro,
and they want me to stand,
Squeeze your butt cheeks they demand,
And I have to get them to understand,
I have been given laxatives so trust me I am.

It says I have a group exercise class from ten to eleven,
On a board above my bed attached to the wall,
I tell my friend Barry it's a Zumba class,
for those who can only crawl,
It is ten past ten and no nurse has come to call,
So he takes it upon himself to go to the nurses' stall,

I hear someone say, "I am sorry sir there's no Zumba, none
at all."
And laughter ringing down the hall.

I always assumed strokes happened to old folk,
But in my first group exercise class I meet Oko,
He was younger than me big and strong,
and looked like he could be an Edmonton Eskimo.
You could be doing everything right, but oh no
So be wary of the signs:
Are your words slurred?
Is your vision blurred?
Does your skin feel like it's falling off your face?
Does an arm feel like you can't move it a trace?
If so, get on the line and call for help and do it in haste,
because time you cannot waste.

Despite the trauma,
It would have been easy to create drama,
Holding a pity party and crying for my momma,
But that wasn't going to help or change my dilemma.

> *'Hope comes in the dark, the stubborn hope that if
> you show up and try to do the right thing, the dawn
> will come. You wait and watch and work: you never
> give up.'*
>
> *- Anne Lamott*

A symptom for stroke survivors is they are naive,
They think they can do more than they can actually achieve,
I was guilty of that before I had a stroke, many people
did perceive,
So I get a visit from my friend Denis L. and a grand plan
I do conceive.

11

I am supposed to have two attendants to transfer me from
my bed to a wheelchair.
My bladder is full and and I weave a plan so I can relieve,
I convince Denis to get me my chair and I will transfer myself
with ease,
He questions my logic as he is not easy to deceive,
A "duh" moment as I forget I am hooked up to all kinds
of monitors,
As I attempt to stand alarms start sounding off,
as if we were breaking into a jewelry store like a couple
of thieves,
He is rushing towards me with the chair in case I tumble,
so I can be safely received.
At the same time nurses come scurrying in,
and he is the guilty party they believe.
As one turns to him and says, "Sir, you have to leave!"
He deals with this calmly not blowing any steam,
He is a good man and old school it would seem,
Because he readily takes this one for the team.
Me? I think it is time for a pee I deem.

It was so humbling to see,
All the wonderful people who went out of their way to visit me.
The hockey community was amazingly good,
Even the players who don't pass to me when they should,
But the white squads I must still attack, in my eyes you will
always be a bunch of hacks.

The loyalty of dear friends like Kathy and Barry who always
has a positive answer,
But not this time as he has his own battle with cancer.
There is a theme here that may be repetitive,
One may get the impression I am a tad competitive.
Let's just say in my younger days playing hockey,

I should have been given a sedative.
My buddy, Barry, was pleased to find,
That I was still sound of mind,
His cancer had been quite a grind,
But I turned to him with mind quite quick,
And said, "I can even beat you at getting sick."
I don't want to give anyone the impression that between my
ears I may be thick,
Cancer patient or stroke survivor? Neither one would I pick.

To the former students who showed how much they cared,
Rekindling powerful and fun moments that we shared,
To dear friends from the present and the past,
Who demonstrated how the power of love can last,
Like the surprise of seeing Peggy and Doug,
Who gave my heart strings a tug,
And to friends and family who reached out from afar.
Oh the woes of technology I would bemoan,
But now l marvel at the capability of a cell phone,
Receiving daily texts from my sister Natalie,
Who after all may not be the black sheep of the family,
But my negative technological rants,
Finds a way to kick me in the pants,
I tell my daughter we should have named her Sunny because
she shines so bright.
Her boyfriend Dan says, "Good thing you didn't because
that's a stripper's name."
So I have to ask, "How would you know?" Trying to instill
some shame.
So one night I think I am texting her and I write, "Sweet
dreams, Sunny"
But I send it to my pal Kelly instead and he replies, "And the
same to you."

I begin to wonder about his calm reaction and think this is
unsettling and funny!
Because I don't want him to think he is my new honey.

To one and all when you get the chance,
Reach out to someone who has fallen on a diffi-
cult circumstance,
For it is a gift that will leave you with a good feeling,
And it could be the spark that leads to positive healing,
For it is in the power in giving,
Which is soul food for the living.

> *'Try to be a rainbow in someone's cloud.'*
> *-Maya Angelou*

I have lived from coast to coast,
And have met some of the finest folk I can proudly boast,
For the many friends I have I feel blessed,
And my childhood ones are some of the best,
As the fond memories that have withstood the test of time
will attest,
And I do not say this next bit in jest.

> *"Many people will walk in and out of your life, but true*
> *friends leave footprints in your heart.'*
> *- Eleanor Roosevelt*

Often when we are knocked down in life we choose to isolate,
Sitting alone to commiserate for what we deem as
a bitter fate,
Do this and you will deteriorate,
It is with human interaction we need to recuperate,
Be the first to initiate,

And warmth in your soul will start to infiltrate
and permeate.

After two weeks I was on the move to the Glenrose,
Whose reputation for rehabilitation just grows and grows.

One of the first people I meet is Frankie at the dinner table,
Who appears to me to be so capable,
His walking seems so stable,
He encourages and reiterates keep working hard and soon
you will be able,
Working hard in therapy, I see growth and know it is not
a fable,
Neither one of us want to go through life disabled,
Or wearing a handicapped label.

Even the left side of my face is affected,
As I notice I am starting to drool,
Gross. On my lap there is a little saliva pool,
Seriously, this is not very cool.

I considered myself an eternal optimist,
Always look for the good I would insist,
But sometimes the darkness calls and I can't resist,
It whispers in my head, no rock climbing, no mountain
scrambling, no hockey, no guitar playing, no performances,
no cycling...
I must force my brain to cease and desist,
For these negative thoughts my ass they can kiss,
Because I have too many things left to do on my bucket list.
And I am still alive,
The challenge is to find a way not just to survive but to thrive,
And we all know the key to any success is inner drive.

I believe things happen for a reason,
But my body has committed treason,
I struggle to understand,
What is God's plan,
I took pride in my ability to inspire,
But I feel like I've lost it with what has transpired.
I meet with Matt, the music man there, one the kindest souls,
I must say who rekindled my fire,
At my website he did look,
And he asked did you ever consider writing a book,
And that's all it took,
So I devote my time,
To writing lines that are filled with rhyme,
To me it all seems so sublime,
Because I don't want to sit around and write,
For I want to go out and play with all my might,
Doing all the things that bring me delight,
And not get stuck having short sight,
I must stay strong and believe I will overcome this plight.

So why the rhymes?
I have done bullying prevention presentations,
And for my Mr. I introduction,
I would start off as a rapper,
Hoping the students would think I was cool and dapper,
How you all doing my name is Mr. I,
I came here today to testify,
And I'll tell you one thing and it aint no lie,
Yo G.I'm pretty fly for a white guy.
Some of you all thinking just look at that old fool,
Trying to drop bombs acting like he cool,
But I bust the rhymes and I break the rules,
Yo Dog, I'm old school.

It always garnered a reaction,
Allowing me to go into a new environment and gain
some traction,
From there I would get into not passing judgement,
Just because someone was different,
Which about now about me would be pretty well every-
one's sentiment.

The nurses on 3A are like representatives from the
United Nations,
Sharing a common bond of care and devotion for
their patients.

> *'If you have much, give of your wealth, if you have
> little, give of your heart.'*
>
> *-Arabian proverb*

Not only does a stroke traumatize and victimize,
But it can dehumanize,
Because even the simplest of task,
For assistance you must ask,
And my frustrations I have to mask.

There is FlorAnn,
Who will do all that she can,
To maintain your dignity as a human.

And there is Cynthia C.who stands tall like an
Princess,
She teaches me how to self dress,
I stumble and I bumble putting things on backwards
I must confess,
But I am getting closer to independence.

And the other Cynthia who is so sweet and shy,
Who one day I had to mortify,
When I have to use the restroom perchance,
I need help with my transfer as I have to hold on to a bar
attached to the commode for balance.
And once there I need to secure a steady stance,
Her role is to make sure I'm steady so I don't shimmy
and dance,
As she assists me I turn to her and say,
"Cynthia it's our first date and you're already pulling down
my pants!"
Did she think I was funny? Not a chance!
As I sit on the commode and finish my wee wee dance,
There is a sign on the wall that I always glance,
It reads pull the call bell for assistance,
For safety is in your hands,
But when I look down I can't help but think,
That what I have in my hands may have different names in
different lands.
But safety? Not a chance!

And Shattel who always conducted herself with such style,
With a morning smile as wide as a mile,
For example, one Monday morning she yelped in delight,
At the sight of Nester who walked into the dining room
upright with only the help of a cane,
A victory for him was a win or us all,
As he entered with a smile and standing tall.

Even though you were betrayed by your body,
They all worked so hard to preserve your sense of dignity,
And my respect and admiration for what they do goes
beyond infinity.

And the therapists were absolutely great,
Pushing us all towards a better fate,
Even though many of us were in a pretty sad state,
We all improved at our own rate,
It didn't take them long to know,
I was rammy and just wanted to go,
Even though I sometimes felt we were going too slow,
Especially with my walking steady improvement I began
to show.

You want to stay on Mona's good side,
As a therapist she is totally bona fide,
Unparallelled expertise she will provide,

And there was Eric the Chill,
Confidence in the patient he would instill,
If there is anything he can do to help, he will,
And Shashi who brought good energy everywhere she went,
because she was so spunky,
I just thought she was funky because she liked my raps.

And Reba who worked on making my core strong,
Every session she would have the radio on,
And everyday like an omen the same song would come on,
From the Imagine Dragons,
"Whatever It Takes" serving as my inspiration.

And my OT therapist Mark who tried everything to get me
to mend,
A session with him was like working out with an old friend.

And to the students Nathan and Taylor learning from the best,
Eager to put their learning to the test,
I know their future patients will feel like they are blessed.

And my therapist Heather,
Who is like a smiling ship in stormy weather,
She hustles all the information she can gather,
So when I leave I can piece my life back together.

It is beyond me how any of these people someone would
want to disparage,
Because all they do is encourage,
They focus on every little gain,
So continued growth you may sustain.

> *'The truest help we can give an afflicted man is not
> to take his burden from him, but to call out his best
> energy, that he may be able to bear the burden.'*
>   *-Phillips Brooks*

It feels like my brain has put my body in jail with no bail,
My daughter videos me taking my first steps with a cane and
it is not a smooth sail,
She posts it on facebook and what an inspiration people hail,
I just see an old man who looks so fragile and frail,
I am now even more determined to prevail,
To make this thing a happy ending tale.

In this situation it is easy to get reflective,
And to put things into a new perspective,
Because the difficult problems I thought I had,
After all weren't really all that bad,
Because when you have your faculties,
You have all the abilities,
To deal with the problems that make you sad,
And to focus on the things that make you glad,
Ask anyone who is ailing and they will tell you that
your health,

Is like possessing precious wealth,
So like the experts say, "Live in the moment and
enjoy yourself."

Never having been one to wrestle with self doubt,
I struggle to understand what this is all about,
Feeling like a boxer who's had his butt kicked in a twelve
round bout,
It would be too easy to mope and pout,
But it is still early so I can't count myself out,
And one day from a mountain top, I shall shout.

I play hockey on Saturdays and Sundays,
And on both skates I am against the white jersey squads,
So in the middle of the night I get an idea I think is bright.
I write poems called The Plight of the White.
I totally throw their players under the bus
and man, does it create a fuss.
I did initiate and instigate
knowing the boys would make some noise and reciprocate.
Here is just a sampling:
Every week the white try their best,
To win one Sunday / Saturday a year is their quest,
Even though this proves to be a most difficult and daunt-
ing test!

I need to share some of their comments with you here,
 because it was done in good cheer
 and what we will all laugh about over a cold beer.
-Pull the plug
-You did do damage to your brain right? Obviously, you need
more medical attention
- And there was the call to decrease or increase the amount
of medication I was receiving.

-Get well. I am hoping to lay some lumber on you soon.
-And my personal favourite "Yep, you are still as dumb
as ever. I was hoping that your brain would get rewired
somehow and I would be able to stand reading your emails."
Of course, there were touching messages of good will but
the best part of any locker room is the banter and the verbal
shots it does instill.

With the help from Tracy I had a session in the pool,
And what a wonderful tool,
I had floaties on and tried to swim,
Kicking my legs but feeling more like a fish with no fin.

Everyone recuperates at their own pace I am told,
Just be patient and positive results will unfold,
But whenever I am told to be patient,
I can't help myself and my standard response is, "I am
a patient!"

We have endured a long winter that much is true,
But now summer is trying to fight through,
Each morning the sky is shining oh so blue,
In my head there's a long list of things I'd love to do,
But right now my options are few,
And one day I will embrace it with joy for I am due.

Today I was promoted with an advancement,
To go to the restroom alone I was declared independent,
In the past If I had to go, I would have to wait for a nurse,
Even if my bladder was going to burst,
But now I can go alone,
To sit on the throne,
To moan and groan all on my own,

To say this brought me contentment,
Would be a huge understatement.

Today, I received a musical treat,
As I get a personal performance from Alexander and Jenessa,
the talented duo known as Jenessia,
As I have always thoroughly enjoy their rhythmic beat,
I want to dance and get up from my wheelchair seat.
The visitors I get make up quite an array,
From amazing musicians,
To Dave and Robert, local politicians,
To former NHL star Eric Christensen who despite
having played on the same teams as Mario Lemieux and
Sidney Crosby,
I keep telling him, "Kid, if I would have been on your line ten
years ago, you really could have gone far!"
Yes quite an array just to see if I'm okay.

We all have to fight to make our lives right,
As with my friend Kelly Falardeau who is a burn survivor,
She has overcome enormous obstacles and is now a thriver,
We have worked together before because her story is
so powerful,
Check out her documentary called Still Beautiful,
If you do you won't regret it,
They actually use one of my songs on the final credits.

> *We shall draw from the heart of suffering itself the*
> *means of inspiration and survival.'*
>   *-Sir Winston Churchill*

So I face the inevitable question how do I cope?
When it feels like I am at the end of my rope,

The answer is always the same, it's hope,
Even though I climb a slippery slope.

> *'Become a possibilitarian. No matter how dark things seem to be or actually are, raise your sights and see possibilities-always see them for they are always there.'*
>
> *-Norman Vincent Peale*

Some days I feel like I am battling with depression,
To motivate myself I steal an expression,
which becomes my new mantra,
And no I didn't steal it from Frank Sinatra,
even though I am doing it my way.
"I am not back yet but I am closer today than
I was yesterday."
Moving forward is what we all need to do, what can I say?

> *'Man performs and engenders so much more than he can or should have to bear. That's how he finds he can bear anything.'*
>
> *-William Faulkner*

Today a new revelation is spawn,
I get a spastic reaction and can raise my arm whenever
I yawn,
So I put the word out for the players on the white squads to
visit me often,
Thinking as they babble and prattle on,
My arm would be moving like a piston.

The time it's taking for my left arm to come around seems
so long,
And people keep telling me I am so mentally strong,
So I accept the challenge of not wanting to prove
anyone wrong,
The last thing I want is to come across as bitter and sour,
But my recovery is going to take more than positive
will power,
So I can one day blossom like a spring flower,
And in my world become an awe inspiring tower,
The key is to keep battling and not become dour.

My wife and daughter have been such pillars of support,
Taking great joy in any progress I would report,
Looking back I realize I was living a blessed life,
Sure I had my share of strife,
But I had a great home with a loving wife.
In a split second, off a precipice my life took a dive,
The bottom line is I am still here,
To that I must give a cheer,
And to move on boldly without any fear,
Or waste my time shedding a tear.

> 'No matter how dark the moment. Love and hope are
> always possible.'
>
> -George Chakiris

The moment I have been waiting for has arrived at last,
For I have been granted a day pass,
Spending it at home with family and friends is such a gas,
Even though it all flew by way too fast,
Winning in euchre was such a blast,
Because Megan and I kicked Dan and Ann Marie's ass!
I don't want to be rude,

But it was great to taste something other than hospital food,
Each bite I thoroughly enjoyed as I slowly chewed,
Dining with family and friends set such a positive mood.
My dog Josie is thrilled beyond belief,
In her eyes you could sense the relief,
It's a good thing I came home though,
Otherwise she would be still staring out the front window,
Wondering why I was a no show.
In a weird way I think she does understand,
Because she constantly tries to nudge my left hand,
It's like she is trying to stimulate movement,
In an attempt to generate some improvement.
And there is Rosie the smallest of the three,
Who feels it is her duty to protect me,
She yips at Bruno who just wants a pet,
Because he doesn't quite get it yet.

Alas I have to return to the scene,
So I can continue with the routine,
To rehabilitate into a well-oiled machine.

I am asked, "Do you think things would have been better off
if you died?"
Of course not I lied,
To my inner self I chide,
Where is your sense of pride,
Do you realize how many tears your daughter and others
would have cried,
I still have a chance to make a difference and that can't
be denied.
I used to say as a coach the easiest thing to do is to quit,
But you won't get any respect, not one bit,
It's time to step up and show some grit,
Time to fight and get on with it.

Having escaped death on previous occasions, I thought
I was invincible,
But now I feel incapable and extremely vulnerable,
I used to take pride doing things with people half my age,
But now I must try to move on and turn the page,
Even though I feel like I am stuck in a cage.

With heartfelt thanks to Danny B.,
I now get weekend passes because he installed railings,
That are super strong and work without failing,
Now the possibility of me returning home is clear sailing.
So I get a weekend pass and all goes smooth minus
one exception,
I need someone to put in my stomach my daily injection,
My wife readily offers her services with no objection,
I upset her earlier in the night and my suspicion came
to fruition,
As she places the needle in my belly, I feel an extra jiggle and
a wiggle,
Despite my yelp, I swear I heard a giggle.

As I struggle with this new situation,
I try indulging in things that will provide motivation.
I read former NFL player, Teddy Bruschi's book, Never Give Up,
a stroke survivor, who played pro football again months
after he suffered a stroke to find inspiration.
I watch Tony Robbins who states,
"It's not what happens to you but what happens FOR you."
For me? Thanks but no thanks. I'm good.
I watch the Secret to reinvigorate,
It stipulates you attract in your life what your
thoughts dictate,
So in my head I orchestrate project regenerate,
Because I know one day I will celebrate.

Even though I find myself in a debacle,
I read book after book of people overcoming obstacles,
And I want to be that type of positive spectacle.

There are moments when I just want to scream,
Because I can't believe this is happening and it's all just
a bad dream.
I loved life and thought mine was supreme,
If and when I get the use of my arm back,
I am going to take it to a new extreme.

As I reflect how my life could have been more perfect,
I think of things I should have done, or things I should
have tried,
As I look back all I can say is, "Don't should on yourself, just
do it!"
Because life is not a spectator sport!

Today I get a new roommate named Tom,
A kind older man,
Who I immediately dub as Tom the Bomb,
He makes a rookie mistake,
As he tries to get out of his wheelchair,
without first applying the brakes.
He slowly plops to the floor,
and what a commotion this does make,
This moment I cannot forsake,
As I have to declare "You really are Tom the Bomb.
You just blew up in your wheelchair!"
What we hear next is a sound that is rare,
For it is the sound of laughter that we share.

I have a meeting with my team to determine my fate,
To discuss my potential discharge date,

It has been close to two months in institutions and it starts
to grate,
Even though the care I have received has been great
beyond debate.
Bad humour I can't afford,
But I feel like I am in front of a parole board,
So I start off by saying I am a changed man,
And in my heart I have found the lord,
Suffice to say no one is bored.
I feel I am ready to go on my way,
To see how this next chapter is going to play,
And we settle on July fourth- Independence Day.

I tell my friend Pat I see light at the end of the tunnel,
His advice for me, "Don't go to the light."

Tomorrow I leave,
And a new future I must weave,
I will find my way I truly believe,
Even though my arm continues to deceive,
With new challenges new plans I must conceive,
Because I feel I have so much more to achieve.

Under the heading of Life is not fair,
A story beyond compare,
My first day on my own,
I go for a walk to get some fresh air,
And to continue with my body repair,
A girl is walking a pit bull,
and not displaying to it much loving care,
My inner voice tells me to beware,
As I approach the dog is lightning fast,
and catches me unaware,
It's teeth it does bare chomping into my bad arm,

as my skin it does tear,
 I do not fall which proves the strength in my leg is there.
Did I mention my therapists were great beyond compare?
Thankfully there is a bench nearby,
As my body goes into shock and I need a chair,
Off to the hospital for more body care.
I am so upset I tell people I want to find the dog and kick it,
I swear,
Seriously, a one armed stroke survivor against a pit bull,
now how would I fare?
At least, I now have an interesting story to share.

As much as this saga seems inane.
The beast yanks so hard on my arm,
My shoulder is in constant pain,
It totally affects my ability to train,
And limits my left arm to make a gain.

When I get my stitches out,
The nurse is a parent from my old school,
I tell her my plan to use this experience to write a book,
so maybe it can serve as a healing tool.
She replies matter of factly. "Well of course."
Like there was no other recourse,
I am taken aback for I never directly taught her daughter,
So I wonder who is her source?
More importantly, it serves to reinforce,
The need to stay the course.

Even though I consider my situation a curse,
My wife reminds me how it could have been so much worse,
For starters, I could have been going for a ride in a hearse,
I see people wearing patches,
because they have lost sight in an eye,

And those who struggle to articulate,
no matter how hard they try,
Some who may never walk again, oh my!

I used to be excitable as a little boy,
But now there are days where it is difficult to find joy,
So these strategies I write about, I must employ,
For what ails me I think I have the cure,
So I organize a mountain hike
and dub it The Road to Recovery Tour.
I am going to enjoy it with family, friends and
former students.
The view from up top is spectacular,
and the joy we embrace on the summit will be so pure.
Will this kick my ass? Of that, I am sure!

> *Things turn out best for the people who make the best*
> *of the way things turn out.*
> *-Art Linkletter*

So Dan and I do some stairs to prepare for the big date,
And the next day my legs are sore,
This is a good thing because two months before,
I couldn't even drag my feet across the floor,
When we are in pain we like to commiserate,
So I find joy Dan is in a similar state,
And to validate this could mean one of two things,
That we have reason to substantiate we did things at
a hard rate,
Or his fitness level, he may need to reevaluate and elevate.
I enjoyed being fit,
Because it motivated me to go after it.
It being anything you wanted to accomplish
because you had the energy to see to it.

I go to outpatient for an assessment,
And for another therapy session,
They remark it is evident I have been on a mission,
Keep fighting hard is the lesson.
And the therapists bring the same thought to mind,
In how they are defined
Each one is so unbelievably kind,
Fighting for each patient regardless who they are assigned

On my daily walk I move at a tortoise's gait,
When I run into friends they exclaim,
"Look at you! You look great!"
But I am used to doing things at an athletic rate,
All I can think is, "Man, I must have looked so bad
when I was knocking on death's gate!"
It is obvious to them I am trying,
and that is something people can and will always appreciate.

There are times I wonder how much more of this I can take,
For the things I love to do I must forsake,
I have to trust this is a temporary break,
And it is a spectacular comeback I will make.

> *The only courage that matters is the kind that gets*
> *you from one moment to the next.*
>   *-Mignon McLaughlin*

It seems recently in my life I've had a propensity to
invite adversity,
For example, how I ended my teaching career was
an absurdity.
Three years ago I destroyed
the ACL, PCL, and MCL ligaments in my left knee,
I fully recuperated by training with intensity,

To the point where I thought I was a hero,
But now I find myself back to ground zero.

I now work with a tens machine,
Ann Marie is experimenting with it acting as the
voltage bringer,
I find myself getting a zinger, you can say a real humdinger,
On the positive side, I find out I am still a singer!

The U of A contacts the Glenrose about having a stroke survi-
vor, speak to the therapy students as a point of reference,
Thankfully I am chosen due to Mona's insistence,
Personally I am thrilled,
because to me this opportunity has significance,
For we are truly alive,
when given the chance to make a positive difference.

Lately I have been having dynamic dreams,
Where I am rock climbing and playing music,
and so realistic it seems.
I hope it means my brain is starting to fire up,
and full recovery is what it deems.

Barry and I go to the under 18 world hockey championships,
It is like old times and what we both need despite
our hardships,
Team Canada takes home the crown,
And I interpret it as a sign good times are coming round,
And our health is gaining ground!

The spiritual experts say,
you have to find a way,
to be able to say, "Today I'm having a good day!"
I knew that,

and I began thinking
that can be easier said than done sometimes.
But today I am happy to say I'm having a good day!
My shoulder was in less pain
so my arm moved with much less sway,
I got into a groove and my arm I was able to move,
For the first time in a very long time,
I was able to lift it over my head,
The first of many I pledged!
They have been working my legs hard in outpatient physio,
On my daily walks I am feeling so strong,
On my walk today I totally knew for sure,
I would be making it to the top during the Road to
Recovery tour,
Because my legs are back!
And that's a fact, Jack!

We either find a way or make one.
- *Hannibal*

I find myself being more emotional,
Which is something I always tried to control,
We go to a concert and when the band starts their set,
The side of my face is all wet,
I just cried,
With all my might I wanted to stop and I tried,
Not wanting to upset my daughter who was by my side,
For I know what it is like to be on stage,
And to have an audience totally engage,
It dawned on me,
that this maybe something again I shall never wage.
Not that I was a big deal,
But performing for me always held great appeal.

'No life is so hard that you can't make it easier by the way you take it.'

- Ellen Glasgow

From the other side of the country,
I get a visit from my sister and brother, Natalie and Stan,
He travels all this distance
so that I can prove yet again that in cribbage I am still the Man!
He attempts to model hope because beat me?
He actually thinks he can...
Really? Keep it together Man!

Now for heaven's sake,
I have to push the Road to Recovery Tour back two weeks
due to the BC fires,
a most difficult decision to make.
I lose to my brother in crib and that just takes the cake...
What does a guy have to do to catch a break?

It has been four months
and with little response the future for my arm seems bleak,
But I am a terrible loser and cannot accept defeat,
So I buy a book called Quantum DNA Healing,
a theory that goes to the drum of a different beat.
I am going to be someone who does good,
Because he did all that he could.

This book is just what I needed,
If you are spiritual I recommend you read it,
Before my siblings leave,
I tell them this will be our last meal as a family
They look concerned as if to say, "Hey!"
Am I implying something bad is coming my way.

I explain we will no longer be genetically linked,
as I am altering my DNA.
Now the scientific community may say that's not okay,
But hey, I am a big proponent
of putting the power of the mind into play.
And whatever it takes to save the day!

I used to think in life I enjoyed a challenge,
 and the chance to overachieve,
But now I find I am giving myself excuses to grieve,
Abandoning what I preached the importance to believe,
I feel embarrassed to go out in public,
Thinking I must have done something wrong,
But people are genuinely happy to see me coming along,
It's funny how we put something in our heads and carry on.

> *'The only disability in life is a bad attitude.'*
> *- Scott Hamilton*

Tomorrow is The Road to Recovery Tour,
The weather forecast is cold and wet,
It is September in the Rockies,
So what did one expect?
It is like life, You get what you get,
Do your best and get on with it,
Moving forward with no regret.
People are making this sound like it is a big deal,
But I need to do this to psychologically heal,
And I am ready to tackle this with zeal.

It is a ten km round trip with considerable elevation gain,
Just far enough to ensure my legs will feel pain.
To me that has appeal,

For mere months before my ride was a chair with wheels,
And being on top is going to feel surreal,
I am very excited to close the deal,
Because I know how great it is going to feel.

Yahoo! On Monday,
I am getting a visit from my childhood friend, Schwartz.
As our friendship is solid like a block of quartz,
For he is one of the world's greatest cohorts,
A friend in need is one he readily supports,
Putting a smile on my face with his witty retorts,
Another one who is rotten in crib I must report,
The many situations over the years,
 with wild stories you don't even need to distort,
I give my wife until Wednesday,
before with the two of us, she is out of sorts.

> 'A good friend is like a four leaf clover, hard to find
> and lucky to have.'
> - Irish proverb

The road to Recovery Tour has come and passed,
And from what I can gather, everyone had a blast,
A day filled with fond memories that are destined to last,
For it was shared with such a wonderful cast,
There were thirty strong who came along.

All week long to the other side I did pray,
Hoping they would send good weather our way...
What can I say?

It proved to be such a beautiful fall day.
People were hailing me as an inspiration,

Considering how months before I was in a very
sorry situation,
But I may have been upstaged by Pete's three year
old daughter,
Brynn who made it to the top proving to be quite
the sensation.

And there was Denis who carried no grudge at all,
Despite me getting him kicked out of a hospital,
For him, it was just as big a feat,
As he's got his own battles with diabetes.

From former students and mom, the Beslers,
Who from this point on will be referred to as the Bestlers,
And to the loyalty of former student Sam who I taught three
years ago in grade four,
Bringing along her mom Christina and grandpa, George.
It was a pity after two months her family moved into the city.
In some people's educational philosophy,
the focus should be on curriculum and technology.
This just goes to prove how
relationship building is still the best methodology.
To Jeremy Crocker,
who must take credit for making this a bigger event,
Who once said,
"If this had to happen to someone, it might as well be you,"
thinking I would trigger a motivational moment
but all I could think of is, "Are you off your rocker?"

To Steven C. who guided me safely down, acting as my own
personal sherpa,
And I would be lyin'
Not to mention how happy and surprised I was
to see his brother Ryan.

And to my long time friend Paul,
Who gave me some of the most positive visits
when I was in the hospital.
To my neighbour Jonelle from across the street,
Whose presence was such a treat,
To my long time buddy Kelly or should I say Sunny,
Who came up with the best line that was so funny.
To ease the pain, he gave me an Advil,
Hoping he gave me the right pill, he said,
"Don't panic if you start seeing the northern lights."
Even though it was in the middle of the afternoon still.

To Bob and Chris,
Who I knew for an event like this they would never miss,
To my long time hockey pal Souchie who always has my back,
Even though I wrote him a rap not cutting him any slack.
"How you all doing his name is Dave Souch, (pro-
nounced such)
We may be down by four but that's not much,
Give him the puck and he'll show you who's clutch,
It's only with the ladies he has no touch."

To Paulina and Jake,
Regardless of the adventure,
I knew they would be eager to partake.
And last but not least to Megan and Dan,
Who did so much to ensure everything went according
to plan,
Even carting champagne to the top making the day grand.
And to those whose names I did not include,
I apologize because you were so important for creating the
positive mood,
I thank you all with heartfelt gratitude,
For making me feel alive and so special.

It is a day I will always fondly recall,
And for the record I did have a fall,
But all the king's horses and all the king's men,
Put me back together again.

When we get to the top,
everyone claps for me and to me it is unbelievable,
And the tears begin to roll,
Making it to the top of a mountain is remarkable,
And it is what I need to heal my soul,
For the first time in a long time I feel like I am whole.

I have literally taken hundreds of students to the top of
this peak,
Hoping to instill the self confidence a young person
does seek,
I now fully grasp the power to which this experience
does speak,
And totally believe my future is bright and not bleak.

> *'I know no more encouraging fact than the
> unquestionable ability of man to elevate his life by
> a conscious endeavour.'*
>   *- Henry David Thoreau*

I wake up in pain,
In a heartbeat I would do it all again,
If you would have said this was possible four months before,
people would assume you were insane.
For I always did maintain,
the difference between ordinary and extraordinary is the
word extra,
So push yourself and watch what in life you shall gain.

A day has gone by and I can't help but feel, so what's next?
Maybe it's time I focus on finishing and promoting this text,
I need to keep moving forward and to figure out the
next step,
Now that I have established a foundation,
How about doing it again as a fundraiser for the Heart and
Stroke Foundation,
And if you are reading this,
Trust me it is an event you won't want to miss.

I would tell students you are a reflection of who your
friends are,
These past few days have proven to have the people in my
life it is my honour,
So to my friends near and far,
Thank you for making me feel like a star.

'Life was meant for good friends and great adventures.'
- Anonymous

Every morning I wake up,
the muscles in my shoulder socket are so sore,
Like there are ligaments that are tore,
I have been on such a good roll lately,
it doesn't hurt as much as before,
Like I have opened a door,
and better things are in store,
Because I will be able to move my arm more.

Whenever I now take a seat to eat,
I notice my dogs lay at my feet,
They don't miss a beat,
Knowing I am messy and may get an unexpected treat.

So today I spoke to the therapy students at the U of A,
 and it went very well,
I was giving them the perspective of a survivor,
because I now have a story to tell.
Their positive response in my head triggered a bell,
Because I thought my days of presenting were now a no go,
Without my guitar I felt like I had lost my mojo,
I can still make a difference and this I must not forego,
Because the "Bamma Ramma Slamma Jamma" is back
and that's a fact Jack!
Dan heads up the EGM Society a bullying preven-
tion organization,
And I told him I didn't think I would be able to do any
more presentations,
I now believe my story can still make a positive impression,
Even though for me it is an ongoing lesson,
And good luck to the therapy students on their
healing mission.

So for now, this is how the story does end,
I wanted it to be that I did totally mend,
And that the lessons from this experience was a godsend,
At this point I cannot pretend
that this is something I could defend,
Because there are still days I feel like
I am being driven around the bend.
But it is getting better I must contend,
So I need to stay positively focused to maintain this trend,
Because I still have goals to attend,
And trust me I totally do intend.

So to all who may have experienced the fall,
And to those who are related to one who had this befall,
Face the challenge and answer the call,
To battle and fight that in your minds you stand tall.

> *'You gain strength, courage and confidence by every experience in which you really stop to look fear in the face.'*
>
> *- Eleanor Roosevelt*

> *'If you are looking for self improvement, join the Bamma Ramma Slamma Jamma movement.'*
>
> *- Mark Ivancic*

About the Author

Mark Ivancic spent 28 years as an educator, teaching not just the curriculum, but the individual. Students in Mark's room learned to value reading, perform calculations, study for exams, and as importantly, they learned that Mark Wanted them to succeed personally and academically.

Besides teaching a homeroom class, Mark developed a series of opportunities for students in his school and beyond focusing on character and responding to life with a positive spirit. His belief in each of us leaving a positive footprint on the world led him to involve himself in efforts such as Band Against Bullying and The Power in Me.

Whether teaching in a classroom or engaging in a presentation, Mr. I. arrived with guitar in hand and a song on his lips. His high energy and warmth reached his target audience to share that message of personal growth. Along with his songs and message, Mark Ivancic brought his humour, leaving his audience with a smile.

The energy that Mark brings to his presentations and teaching is also a part of his personal lifestyle. His workouts in the gym created a new peer group with whom he can share his positive message. The former university hockey player loves that game and the character of those that he meets in the dressing room affirms his own desire to leave a footprint that lifts people up. Mark has always been drawn to the mountains and finding his way to the peak an exhilarating experience. Whether scrambling or rock climbing, Mark loves the physical and mental challenge.

Those of us who know him personally know of his resilience, his positivity, his creativity, his passion, and his dogged determination.

Mark's latest effort in personal growth came following a life altering event in his own life: a stroke. While in physical therapy, he arrived at the conclusion that he could write about the experience as an effort to heal himself. His desire to build something positive for himself and for others led to his poetic offerings.

About the author written by great friend Barry Gibson

Family photo at our favorite place, Jasper Lake

Winning a tournament in Victoria last winter. Notice all the bald dudes are placed in the back row far left corner. I am not sure why but I suspect it had something to do with lighting concerns.

Performing at a fundraiser I organized for Bands Against Bullying in support of Bullying Prevention in youth

If you are going to be a Marvel Super Hero, you need a cameo appearance from Stan Lee, in this case my buddy Kelly.

Living life large with my daughter Megan

**Rock climbing in Europe in the
beautiful country of Slovenia.**

In my 40s and learning how to ice climb.